TRANSFORMATIONAL LIFESKILLS PRESENTS

THE VICTIM ADDICTION JOURNAL

30 DAYS THROUGH SELF DISCOVERY

CHANGE THE WAY YOU FEEL ABOUT YOUR LIFE & YOUR LIFE WILL CHANGE

VICTORIA LEE CARLYLE

The Victim Addiction: Thirty Days Through Self-Discovery Journal

ISBN-10:1-943253-10-2

ISBN-13:978-1-943253-10-4

Printed in the United States. Editing: Jana Lee Cox

Publishing: Transformational Life Publishing

Cover art: Brittney Hansen

Cover design and illustrations: Bonilla Design

Book layout and design: Victoria Lee Carlyle: Transformational Life Publishing

Release Date: January 2017

This journal has been provided to assist you in consciously walking through the emotional habits of your mind. As you go through each day you may notice that some of the questions seem repetitious. The purpose for this repetition is to create a familiar pattern that will give you the ability to consciously tap into as many thoughts, feelings, attitudes and beliefs as you can. Trying to process every question available to you will become overwhelming. Choose one or two to work on per day and remember, you can always go back and work through other questions whenever you want so take it slow and enjoy the journey. As your working through the processes you may also find that some of the subjects and processes elicit a strong emotional reaction. A strong reaction just means you have been emotionally wounded, and what is surfacing to a conscious level needs your thoughtful attention.

The questions and processes throughout this book have been designed to help you redirect the neurological configurations and linguistic structures that form the emotional habits of your mind so you can create profound changes easily and quickly. When working through emotions it is vitally important that you get curious with your emotional reactions, and not critical with the discoveries that you make. You have all the power that you need to make profound changes that will enhance a life time of happiness and growth.

The Discovery Begins

The Discovery Begins

- What thoughts frequently surface when I am hurt or offended? *(Why does this always happen to me? I knew I shouldn't have. They should understand how I feel. I've never been good at…)*
- How do I feel when these thoughts surface?
- What attitudes accompany these thoughts and feelings? *(I'm tired of everyone judging me. It's their own fault. Why do I always do this?)*
- What behaviors do I display when these attitudes are present?
- What uncomfortable beliefs validate my behavior? (*I've been hurt, and I'm frightened that if I get hurt again I won't be able to handle it and I'll fall apart. Therefore, I push people away and continue to feel as if "I am not lovable"*)
- How do the cycles *(repetitious thoughts, feelings, attitudes and beliefs)* that come from my emotional perceptions *(a perception based on feelings, not reality)* affect my relationships?
- What are the important relationships in my life?
- How does a meaningful life look for me?

1.

2.

3.

Self-Discovery Notes

Day One

The Road to Emotional Health

The Road to Emotional Health

Spend the next 24 hours answering a few simple questions.

- What makes me happy?
- How does my happiness depend on others, and in what ways am I independently happy with myself?
- In what areas of my life do I seek advice from others?
- In what circumstances or in what emotional "place" do I trust the decisions that I make?
- How would I describe the person I have always dreamed of becoming?
- How has fear sabotaged the person I desire to become?
- What limited beliefs about myself get in the way of my personal progression? *(This is never going to work. I'm not good at__________. What if __________?)*
- On what in my life do I place the most value? *(Health, relationships, career…)*
- For what am I most grateful?
- What am I willing to change in my life to live the life I have always wanted?

Based on the information I have gained, I will take these three actions to strengthen my relationships and make my life more meaningful.

1. ____________________

2. ____________________

3. ____________________

Self-Discovery Notes

Day Two

The Journey Begins

Observing My Emotional Reactions

The purpose of this process is to notice the automatic reactions that occur in your everyday life.

Here is a little experiment to enhance your awareness:

As you read the newspaper or watch the news on TV, notice your emotional fluxes or variations—notice which news stories impact your thoughts and feelings or tap into your memories or beliefs. Also, notice when your mind throws out thoughts that seems illogical or irrational? Pay attention to the intensity of your reactions *(how strong your emotions feel)* and determine if that intensity is appropriate for your current situation.

Choose one scenario where you noticed a reaction and specifically decipher the impact your emotional fluxes have on the way you think, feel, and act.

> When my boyfriend/girlfriend broke up with me I was angry. *(Automatic reaction)* I thought that the reason he/she broke up with me was because he/she was seeing someone else *(My story based on the way I felt, not verifiable facts)*. Because I thought he/she was seeing someone else I felt like I was not good enough for him/her *(The belief based on the story I had made up)*. The first thing I did was call a friend for advice *(My behavior/seeking allies to confirm that my thoughts, feelings, attitudes and beliefs about the scenario are right)*. My friend reminded me that my boyfriend's/girlfriend's last three relationships ended after three months *(Details or facts I overlooked getting into the relationship)*. I felt like

my friend was irritated with me so I quickly said goodbye *(How I projected my feelings on to someone else).* After I got over being mad I was extremely *(the intensity of my emotions)* sad *(How I really felt)* and had a hard time moving on. What I have realized is that the intensity of my sadness was not from my three-month relationship. Rather, it was from all the times I felt abandoned by men/women who have walked out of my life *(My emotional history).*

- What was my automatic reaction?
- What was the story I told myself?
- How does my story influence my perceptions? *(How does what I make up eliminate or alter the facts of what is happening)*
- What belief did I have about the situation?
- What red flags did I overlook when I was getting into the relationship?
- How did I project the way I was feeling on to someone else? *(I felt frustrated so believed others were frustrated with me.)*
- How intense were my emotions?
- How does my history intensify my reaction?
- When my automatic reaction was gone how did I feel? *(Hurt, betrayed, abandoned, left out, lied to.)*
- What do I wish I could change?

Based on the information I have gained, I will take these three actions to understand my reactions, strengthen my relationships, and make my life more meaningful.

1. ____

____

2.

3.

Self-Discovery Notes

Day Three

Emotional Circuitry

Examining My Emotional Circuitry

The purpose of this process is to pay attention to the Emotional Circuitry that alters your physical or emotional well-being.

Several times a day, perhaps on the hour, every hour, write down the way you feel. Pay particular attention to your body's reaction to external stimuli. For example, notice how your body feels. Are your shoulders tight? Are your eyes heavy? Notice your breathing, heart rate, posture, etc.

Throughout the day notice where your thoughts are focused.

- What thoughts make my energy rise?
- What thoughts bring my energy down?
- When I am feeling down, what familiar behavioral patterns do I notice? *(I get angry; I get hurt and go quiet.)*
- This is what I notice about myself when I am having an emotional conversation _________. (*Meeting with my boss; At lunch with friends; Arguing with my child; etc.)*
- What circumstances in my life affect my mood? (*When I am in debt and there is not enough money to pay monthly expenses; When I have too many obligations and can't keep up.)*
- When I think about _________ *(i.e. being in debt)* I go from feeling _________ to _________ *(i.e. calm to tense; happy to sad; frustrated to angry.)*

- When does my emotional shift take place? (*Before I talk to my spouse; During a conversation with my boss; After I have lunch with my friends.)*
- What reoccurring patterns do I notice? *(i.e. Reoccurring thoughts/ things that I make up; Reoccurring circumstances/things that I experience; Reoccurring feelings, reactions or behaviors; Reoccurring attitudes/ things I think about myself or others)*

Based on the information I have gained, I will take these three actions to increase my emotional well-being, strengthen my relationships, and make my life more meaningful.

1. ____

2. ____

3.

Self-Discovery Notes

Day Four

The Victim Addiction

The Victim Addiction

The purpose of this process is to notice the unconscious ways you give your power away to The Victim Addiction.

Take time to notice how prevalent The Victim Addiction is in the world around you. Document the victim statements you say, as well as those you hear; such as, *"It wasn't my fault," "I didn't do it," "What else was I supposed to do?"* etc.

- What language do I use when I feel mistreated or accused, or blame others for my circumstances? *("You make me so mad"; "I get frustrated when you do that.")*
- When and in what ways do I blame myself?
- When and in what ways do I blame others?
- What stories have I made up/created to justify my feelings? *("I've never been good in new situations"; "Why do people always treat me like this?")*
- What is the underlying meaning behind my behaviors and beliefs? *(I've been hurt so I push people away and validate the belief that I am damaged, unworthy of love, or not good enough.)*

Based on the information I have gained, I will take these three actions to notice the unconscious ways I give my power away, strengthen my relationships, and make my life more meaningful.

1. ____

2. ____

3. ____

Self-Discovery Notes

Day Five

False Evidence Appearing Relevant

Identify My Fears

The purpose of this process is to notice the unconscious fears that block your progression and affect your emotional well-being. Some of the fears that limit our ability to think logically include:

- Fear of failure
- Fear of rejection
- Fear of loss
- Fear of changes
- Fear of judgment
- Fear of humiliation
- Fear of being alone
- Fear of being hurt
- Fear of the unknown

Spend the next 24 hours noticing your fears.

- What is the most frightening experience I have ever had?
- Where do I feel the safest?
- What fears do I have around other people?
- When is a time in my life where I let fear hold me back?
- What is my greatest fear with my __________ ? *(self, family, relationship, job, education, faith, future, etc.)*
- I fear this because__________?
- When I am driven by fear, I typically __________ *(Get anxious and push back. Push people away.)*

- In what areas of my life do I let fear limit my ability to make decisions? *(i.e. I hesitate to share my opinion for fear of ridicule, judgment, or rejection.)*
- What stories or rationalizations have I created to cover my fears and justify my reactions?
- What specific steps have I taken to successfully push past my fears and accomplish my desired outcome? (*Identify how you felt about your final objective, how you talked to yourself and others about what and how you wanted, the attitudes you formed to persevere through your doubts, and the beliefs you had regarding your abilities.)*

Based on the information I have gained, I will take these three actions to overcome my fears, strengthen my relationships, and make my life more meaningful.

1. ______________________________

2. ______________________________

3.

Self-Discovery Notes

Day Six

Emotions That Limit Our Growth

Calmly Communicating When Emotions Take Over

The purpose of this process is to think clearly when life feels out of your ability to manage, control, or change.

When emotions take over, give yourself time to cool down before you speak, then consider these questions:

- How do I criticize or blame myself?
- How do I criticize or blame others?
- When I disagree with something, how do I typically respond? *(I get angry and make others wrong. I gather allies who will agree with me.)*
- What "I" statements do I use to describe how I behave in a conflict? *("I get irritated when you interrupt me." "You never listen to me." "We never resolve anything.")*

To effectively communicate what it is you want to say, you will need to identify the source of your feelings and clarify your thoughts. The following questions should help:

- How do I blame others for the way I feel about myself?
- When I struggle, what assumptions do I make about those around me?
- What habits do I use to hide or compensate for my emotions? *(Fight to be right; Withdraw; Smoke; Drink; Overeat; Sleep; Lie.)*

- How can I reframe my self-talk in a conflict to take ownership for my feelings? *(i.e. "When you interrupt me I feel like you are focused on how to fix me rather than trying to understand how I feel or listening to what I am really saying.")*
- Where do I find courage to ask for what I want? *(i.e. Past successes in communication; Confidence in other areas of my life.)*
- How can I transfer that courage to other areas of my life?

Based on the information I have gained, I will take these three actions to increase my ability to effectively communicate, strengthen my relationships, and make my life more meaningful.

1. ______________________________

2. ______________________________

3. ________________________________

Self-Discovery Notes ________________________________

Day Seven

A Life of Pain

The Writing Escape

The purpose of this process is to discover the benefit of tracking familiar emotional cycles that sabotage your ability to succeed.

Keep a mood journal.

It's important that you don't make yourself feel wrong. Feelings are a natural part of the human experience and can be overwhelming and confusing.

If you are struggling with your thoughts, you may want to put a logical answer to some of the questions that run through your mind, such as, "What is wrong with me?" "Why am I feeling this way?" "What do others think of me?" Honestly answering questions like these will help you clarify your thoughts and feelings and relieve pressure you are feeling.

- What thoughts cause overwhelming feelings of despair? *(i.e. What if I lose my job? I can't do this on my own. I'm sure that others would be better off without me.)*
- How do I cope with these thoughts and the feelings that go with them?
- Who is part of my support system?
- Whom do I trust with my deepest thoughts?
- How do I compare myself to others?
- In what areas of my life do I know that I am enough?
- When I struggle, in what ways do I share my thoughts and feelings with others? How do I feel about my approach?

- What do I yearn for people to see in me?
- What can I change so others will see the person I really am?

Based on the information I have gained, I will take these three actions to understand the emotional cycles that keep me down, strengthen my relationships, and make my life more meaningful.

1. ______________________________

2. ______________________________

3. ______________________________

Self-Discovery Notes

Day Eight

Emotional Validation

Emotional Validation

The purpose of this process is to become familiar with the emotional and physiological reactions caused by emotional perceptions.

To begin the process, it is important to identify where you are.

- I am curious as to why _________. *(I always react when people raise their voice. People always see the worst in me. Talking to my dad really gets me down.)*
- When _________ *(what I have named)* occurs, my thoughts are?
- And I feel _________.
- What story do I tell myself about the situation?
- What automatic assumptions do I make from the story I created?
- What decisions did I make, or ponder making, based on the way I felt?
- What are my beliefs around _________?
- How do my emotional perceptions regarding _________ affect my behavior?
- How do my emotional perceptions validate my feelings? *(I am under a lot of pressure and get frustrated with others over simple things.)*
- What physical symptoms do I notice when I am emotional? *(I feel anxious. My heart races. My head aches. I feel fatigued.)*

- How do my emotional perceptions distort a realistic view of myself or others?

Based on the information I have gained, I will take these three actions to increase my awareness, strengthen my relationships and make my life more meaningful.

1. ______________________________

2. ______________________________

3. ______________________________

Self-Discovery Notes

Day Nine

Between Stimulus and Response

Between Stimulus and Response

The purpose of this process is to disrupt the stimulus that prevents a conscious response.

Begin by interrupting your automatic urge to act by observing how your thoughts, feelings, attitudes, and beliefs influence your behavior in the simple scenarios that occur throughout the day.

Consciously note what is going on before you take any action.

Notice how your mind analyzes a situation when you are emotional, vs. what is realistically going on. Imagine a neutral third party perspective.

- When I am upset, how does what I see intensify the situation? *(He raised his hand to block the sun and I assumed he made a crude gesture. Her raised eyebrow made me feel she questioned my knowledge.)*
- When I am upset, how does what I hear intensify the situation? *(including voice tone and fluctuation)*
- When I am upset, how do my feelings amplify the situation?
- When I am upset, how do the stories I form persuade my emotional justifications?
- When I am upset, how do the stories I form validate that what I am feeling is non-biased reality?
- When I am upset, how do my attitudes intensify the situation beyond what is real? *(I am so tired of being treated like this)*

- How have my emotional interpretations affected my behavior? *(I become angry and lose control; My defenses go up and I distance myself.)*
- How have my emotional interpretations affected the way I feel about myself? (*I knew this was never going to work, so why try? Why am I such a loser?)*
- How have my emotional interpretations affected the way I feel about others? (That guy is a real jerk.)
- How will analyzing the emotional components of an emotional situation help me view that situation differently?

Based on the information I have gained, I will take these three actions to increase self-control, strengthen my relationships, and make my life more meaningful.

1. ______________________________

2. ______________________________

3.

Self-Discovery Notes

Day Ten

Our Comfort Zone

Viewing Our Comfort Zone

This process is designed to help you notice areas in your life where your comfort zone limits your ability to create successful outcomes.

- What do I notice about my comfort zone?
- What illusions do my Comfort Zone create? (*I stay at a job with little chance of advancement. I stay in an unhappy relationship. I live in a home that I don't like.*)
- What types of fear keep me in my comfort zone? *(Fear of failure, fear of rejection, fear of criticism.)*
- What do I fear will happen if I step outside of my comfort zone?
- What reoccurring thoughts keep me in this fearful place?
- How does familiarity create safety that keeps me in my comfort zone? *(I'm lonely but prefer to stay at home by myself)*

Now examine other patterns that keep you in your comfort zone.

- What common mistakes do I make in relationships?
- What is my deepest regret?
- What are my secret insecurities?
- What judgments do I fear the most?
- What pushes me into my comfort zone and what pulls me out?

Based on the information I have gained, I will take these three actions to get out of my comfort zone, strengthen my relationships, and make my life more meaningful.

1. ______________________________

2. ______________________________

3. ______________________________

Self-Discovery Notes

Day Eleven

The Road to Self-Discovery

Self-Discovery

The purpose of this process is to create lasting change by clarifying the impact of your emotional well-being when you feel uncomfortable, acknowledge your coping strategies, and define the exceptional qualities that make you unique.

Identify areas in your life where you feel outside of your ability to manage, control, or change your circumstance.

- How do my emotions affect my physical wellbeing? *(When I argue with my sister, my jaw aches from clenching my teeth, my hands sweat, and my head usually aches.)*
- What is my typical behavior when I feel outside my ability to manage, control, or change my circumstance? *(I get frustrated, I figure it out, I ask for help, I fight to be right, I withdraw.)*
- What do I notice about my mood when I feel outside my ability to manage, control, or change my circumstance? *(After talking with my boss, I feel inadequate, and my posture, confidence, mood drastically change)*
- How do my emotions reflect in my body language? *(When I first sit down with my sister I am happy, but when she starts talking about my marital problems I sit up immediately and become exasperated and angry.)*
- I feel as if others are _________ . *(judging, blaming, accusing me)*
- My *story* is _________. *(After talking to my son, I feel irritated and I think to myself, I do so much for him. Why can't he just do what I ask?)*

- When I feel outside my ability to manage, control, or change my circumstance what is the kindest thing I can do for myself?
- When I am overwhelmed, what is the kindest thing others can do for me.
- Where do I ask for help or from whom?
- What is the hardest challenge I have ever overcome?
- How has overcoming that challenge impacted my life?
- What is causing me the most stress right now?
- What am I doing to resolve the stress in my life?

Each of us has automatic coping strategies that help us maneuver through emotional times. A few common strategies include getting angry, exaggerating / lying, hiding, overeating, oversleeping, or "medicating" with drugs or alcohol.

Take a moment to think about the automatic strategies you use when you have an emotional encounter.

- What are my common coping strategies?
- In what circumstances do I notice these strategies?
- What situations cause me to feel defensive?
- What coping strategies do I use when I feel defensive?
- Do I consider myself to be a person who contributes to the wellbeing of others or do I manipulate others to get what I want? How do I contribute? How do I manipulate?

Now shift your focus to acknowledge some of the wonderful attributes that make you unique.

- What are my three greatest strengths?
- What things do I enjoy most about myself?
- What things do I enjoy most about my life?

- What would I do if I knew I could not fail?
- What experience taught me my greatest lesson?
- What is my greatest personal accomplishment?
- What is the nicest compliment I have received?
- What excites me about the future?
- What have I always wanted to do?
- What is the number one thing I hope to accomplish in my life?
- How do I celebrate my accomplishments?

Based on the information I have gained, I will take these three actions to acknowledge my gifts, strengthen my relationships, and make my life more meaningful.

1. ______________________________

2. ______________________________

3.

Self-Discovery Notes

Day Twelve

Developing our Experiences

Understanding our Experiences

The purpose of this process is to clarify how familiar emotional experiences alter your perceptions.

- When was the last time I had an emotional reaction?
- What triggered that reaction?
- What felt out of my power to control? *(_________ was so angry that he/she wouldn't listen and there was nothing I could do about it.)*
- What thoughts and feelings surfaced around this interaction?
- What memories surfaced? *("I wasn't good enough for this person." "I tried that and it failed." "I don't want to get hurt again"; etc.)*
- How did those memories help to validate my feelings?
- What prominent beliefs were tied to my reaction?
- What fears intensified my reaction?
- In what ways, did I justify my behavior or fight to be right?
- What are some of the stories I tell myself to justify my emotional reality surrounding this event and reoccurring emotional reactions?
- What's typical about my story or reaction?
- How do my reactions affect my relationships?

Now take time to analyze your emotional reactions.

- What emotions do I often feel?
- What meaning do I typically attach to these familiar feelings?
- How do my thoughts give validation to the way I am feeling?

- What types of thoughts affect my mood?
- How does struggling to do something right, making a mistake, or receiving disapproval from others affect the way I feel about myself?
- Who do I feel always judges me?
- How do their judgments make me feel about myself or my abilities?
- What stories have I created *(about myself or others)* around these feelings?
- How do I communicate when I feel uncomfortable?
- How do I communicate when I don't get what I want?
- How do my unspoken communications affect the relationships in my life? (i.e. voice inflection, body language, facial expression)

Based on the information I have gained, I will take these three actions to understand my perceptions, strengthen my relationships, and make my life more meaningful.

1. ______________________________

2. ______________________________

3.

Self-Discovery Notes

Day Thirteen

The Impact of Our Thoughts

Getting Curious with Self-Talk

The purpose of this process is to help you notice where you place your energy by looking at your self-talk.

At least three times a day, consciously notice the subjects you are thinking about. Are you associating your emotional energy with things that build you up or on little things that bring you down? Create a list of your thoughts. Let's call the uplifting thoughts our Fantabulous List, and the list of those thoughts that bring us down or discourage us our Craptacular List.

Fantabulous List

Craptacular List

Keep in mind that your Craptacular thoughts should never be ignored or overlooked. These thoughts will be a valuable benchmark in noticing the gap between where you are and where you want to be.

As you write these lists, you may experience illogical feelings. If this occurs just know that these feelings are tapping into other times in your life where your felt uncomfortable or experienced emotional pain. Notice when these types of feelings prevent you from making changes or taking risks.

Fantabulous	Craptacular

Based on the information I have gained, I will take these three actions to encourage uplifting thoughts, strengthen the relationship I have with myself and make my life more meaningful.

1.

2.

3.

Self-Discovery Notes

Day Fourteen

The Blame Game

Defining the Impact of Blame

The purpose of this process is to identify areas in your life where blame is taking your personal power and compromising your relationships.

- What is the impact of blame on the relationships in my life?
- Are there areas in my life where I make excuses or take responsibility for the misdeeds of others *(parents, siblings, spouse, children, etc.)*
- In what areas of my life have I transferred my angst by making excuses that justify my poor/negative actions?
- When might I blame others for the things I don't like about my life or myself?
- When might I blame others for the things I am unwilling to change?
- For what actions or feelings do I need to forgive myself?
- To whom should I apologize for the ways I have blamed them?
- What fears do I have of apologizing or asking for forgiveness?
- In what other areas of my life do I resist shedding hurtful feelings?

For those suffering with blame, guilt or resentment:

- How long have I been holding on to this guilt and/or resentment?
- How does blaming others make me feel? *(validated, justified, right)*

- What price have I paid for my blame?
- What price have others paid for my blame?
- How does blame affect the way I feel about myself?
- How is blaming others cutting me off from the love and understanding I want to receive?

For those suffering from secrets and lies:

- What am I hiding?
- Why have I held on to this secret/lie for so long?
- Why am I afraid to reveal my secrets/lies?
- What personal price have I paid for holding on to my secrets/lies?
- For what do I blame myself?
- How have I justified withholding information related to the mistakes I have made?
- In what ways have I concealed my secrets/lies from others?
- Who have my secrets and lies hurt?
- I have a hard time being honest with __________ because __________ .
- How has holding secrets affected the level of trust I have in myself?
- What am I failing to accept about myself?
- What am I worried people will think if I am honest about the secrets I have concealed?
- What am I afraid of losing?
- How have secrets affected the level of trust I have for those around me?
- In what ways have I held on to my secrets and pushed others away?

Based on the information I have gained, I will take these three actions to let go of blame, strengthen my relationships, and make my life more meaningful.

1. ______________________________

2. ______________________________

3. ______________________________

Self-Discovery Notes

Day Fifteen

Unconscious Attitudes & Assumptions

Defining Attitudes & Assumptions

The purpose of this process is to listen for attitudes and assumptions that get in the way of your happiness and growth.

- What attitudes and assumptions have I formed about people in my life?
- What stories do I tell myself to support my attitudes and assumptions?
- What beliefs give support to my attitudes and assumptions? *(They should listen. This always happens to me.)*
- How have my attitudes and assumptions increased my insecurities and fears?
- What effect have my attitudes and assumptions had on my relationships? *(I don't think people like me so I push them away before they can hurt me.)*
- How have my attitudes and assumptions prevented me from accomplishing my goals?

Based on the information I have gained, I will take these three actions to change the attitudes and assumptions that get in the way of loving relationships and creating a more meaningful life.

1. ______________________________

____

____

2.

3.

Self-Discovery Notes

Day Sixteen

Forming Our Belief System

Noticing Our Belief System

The purpose of this process is to open the door of awareness by noticing the emotional beliefs that control your behaviors.

- What is the most debilitating belief I have about myself?
- What is the most debilitating belief I have about others? *(No one supports me. No one understands how hard I try.)*
- What belief is behind my sabotaging self-talk? *(I'm not valued, I'm not good enough…)*
- How have beliefs like these compromised my confidence?
- What impact have beliefs like these had on my relationships? What beliefs are behind my feelings of disappointment, guilt, or fear?
- What fear-based stories do I tell myself? *(Example: I have to make a certain amount of money before I can socialize, get married, or have a child)*
- What belief is behind that fear? *(I won't fit in, be accepted, or have the ability to provide.)*
- What are some of the ineffective habits I have developed because of my beliefs? *(i.e. I've never been good at __________ so I don't feel comfortable __________)*

Strengthening Empowering Beliefs

This process will help you strengthen the neural pathways that support the changes you want to make. Because this process is done with your eyes closed, it is easier to have someone to guide you. Or, you can write out the process and record the words, giving you the necessary time to pause and reflect. Either way, the point is to focus your attention on what you feel. Begin the process by thoughtfully pondering the following outline.

I would like to improve _________ *(Example: my social skills).*

Now think of a memory where you felt entirely _________ . *(Example: socially accepted. It could be as simple as how accepted you felt when you went to work with your father or visited your grandmother.)*

While thinking of that memory, take a breath and connect to the way it felt to feel completely _________ *(accepted).* While breathing in, tighten your fists to enhance feelings of your _________ *(acceptance)* even deeper. As you inhale, feel the power of _________ *(being accepted)* run through your body. Continue tightening and releasing your fists until you are fully connected to all the _________ *(acceptance)* you want to experience. Breathe in several times while repeating 10 times "I am _________ *(accepted).*

Now, continue this process by connecting what you would like to improve to an empowering "I am" belief. *(I am powerful; I am courageous; I am valuable; I am important)*

I would like to improve _________ *(social skills).* A belief that will increase my abilities is _________ *(I am confident).*

Once you have chosen an area you want to improve and have formulated a belief that you would like to enhance, close your eyes and connect to a time in your life where you felt completely *(name the belief)* _________ *(Example: Confident.*

Confidence may be as simple as remembering how you felt the first time you rode your bike by yourself, got an "A" on a school report, or gave a successful presentation).

Now, think of a memory where you felt entirely _________ *(confident).*

While thinking of that memory, take a breath and connect to the way it felt to feel completely _________ *(confident).* While breathing in, tighten your fists to enhance feelings of _________ *(confidence)* even deeper. As you inhale, feel the power of _________ *(confidence)* run through your body. Continue tightening and releasing your fists until you are fully connected to all the _________ *(confidence)* you want to experience. Breathe in several times while repeating 10 times "I am _________ (confident)." Feel how good it feels to be that _________ *(confident).*

Now let's bring the feeling of being _________ and the belief of _________ together.

Think of a time when you felt _________ and _________.

While thinking of that memory, take a breath and connect to a time when you were _________ and felt _________. (*I felt socially accepted and felt confident. It could be as simple as when you made your first friend in kindergarten.*)

As you inhale, connect to the power that already exists in the memories of being _________ *(accepted)* and feeling _________ *(confident).* While breathing in, tighten your fists to enhance your feelings of _________ and your belief of _________ *(acceptance and confidence)* to anchor these feelings even deeper. Continue tightening and releasing your fists until you are fully connected to all the _________ and the belief of _________ *(acceptance and confidence)* you want to experience. Breathe in several times while repeating 10 times "I am _________ and _________ *(socially accepted and confident).* Feel how good it feels to be that _________ and _________ *(socially accepted and confident).*

Now that you have anchored the skill to a strong belief, think of a scenario where you can utilize your new skill and the belief that goes with it. With your eyes closed imagine all the support you are getting from others. Hear the excitement in others' voices as they respond to your _________ and _________. Feel how wonderful it feels to use your new skills to enhance every area of your life.

Now take a deep breath to complete the anchor, and, when you are ready, open your eyes.

Throughout the week breathe in several times while repeating 10 times, "I am _________ and feel _________.

Use this process anytime you want to improve your skills or enhance your performance.

Based on the information I have gained, I will take these three actions to change the attitudes and assumptions that get in the way of loving relationships and creating a more meaningful life.

1. ____

____

____

____

2.

3.

Self-Discovery Notes

Day Seventeen

Emotional Associations

Emotional Associations

The purpose of this process is to help you take a neutral look at the emotional associations you have formed throughout your life.

Think of a time in your life where you felt mistreated or misunderstood. Play the scenario over in your mind as if you were an observer. Try to notice the emotional association you have regarding the interaction.

From a neutral place, take a look at what occurred.

- What did I observe about myself?
- What did I observe about others?
- What was actually said?
- How did I change the facts to validate my perception?
- What did I make up about the physical or emotional reactions of others? *(i.e., body language, facial features, posture, voice fluctuation, pitch, tone.)*
- What feelings did I add to the conflict?
- How did my history intensify my experience?
- What facts did I overlook in order to validate my history?
- On what should I seek clarification?
- Of what and to whom should I forgive? *(myself or others)*
- What is a more accurate perception of this interaction?

Based on the information I have gained, I will take these three actions to question my stories, strengthen my relationships, and make my life more meaningful.

1. ____

2. ____

3. ____

Self-Discovery Notes

Day Eighteen

Identifying Intensity and Expressing Emotions

Identifying the Intensity of Emotions

The purpose of this process is to notice and identify the intensity of emotional patterns.

At least three times a day for the next week, track the intensity of your emotions. Include the intensity of any irrational thoughts, feelings, or reactions. Wait until the emotions have calmed before you begin the evaluation process.

Use a scale of one to ten; one being least intense and ten being extremely intense.

least intense — extremely intense

○	○	○	○	○	○	○	○	○	○
1	2	3	4	5	6	7	8	9	10

Rate the intensity of your emotional responses. Rating the intensity of your reactions will give you a better understanding of when you are logically dealing with facts versus when you are simply reacting to emotions.

Example:

You are driving in your car and see lights flashing behind you. You look down and notice that your car is going faster than you had realized. Define what runs through your mind and evaluate the intensity of your feelings. Notice if you automatically begin blaming another for your emotional reaction or circumstances.

When you encounter a reaction where your feelings seem intense, take time to process your experience.

Use a scale of one to ten; one being least intense and ten being extremely intense.

least intense									extremely intense
○	○	○	○	○	○	○	○	○	○
1	2	3	4	5	6	7	8	9	10

- What occurred to cause an intense reaction?
- How was this incident similar to other past experiences?
- What was I feeling?
- When have I felt this way before?
- Where did my reaction take my thoughts?
- How has my emotional perception affected my behavior?

This process is for those who struggle with the ability to label or express their feelings.

Learning how to identify our feelings and effectively express ourselves is essential to our happiness and growth.

The best way to begin feeling comfortable with your emotions is to start by identifying feelings around things that you enjoy.

Start by reading the list of beneficial feelings and choosing words that describe your personality, then, look for ways you display those qualities in your life. Or, think of something you currently enjoy or would like to enjoy, then, go to the list below and read the words out loud. Identify the words that best describe emotions of what you enjoy and put them in a sentence that accurately communicates your feelings. *(I think kick boxing is an exhilarating sport! Remodeling things in my home so they are the way I like them is exciting!)*

Beneficial Feelings

Admired	Adventurous	Alive
Ambitious	Balanced	Bold
Brave	Confident	Connected
Content	Courageous	Determined
Dynamic	Eager	Encouraged
Engaged	Enthusiastic	Fabulous
Fantastic	Fascinated	Free-Spirited
Generous	Gratified	Grounded
Happy	Healthy	Honored
Hopeful	Humble	Independent
Innovative	Inspired	Invigorated
Lovable	Loved	Loving
Lucky	Marvelous	Motivated
Overjoyed	Passionate	Peaceful
Perceptive	Productive	Reliable
Reassured	Relaxed	Respected
Satisfied	Secure	Sensational
Successful	Sure	Tenacious
Thankful	Thoughtful	Touched
Upbeat	Unique	Useful
Understood	Valued	Valuable
Willing	Worthy	Worth It

Once you feel comfortable labeling and expressing your pleasant feelings you can move on to describe feelings that are a little less comfortable to express. Begin with simple emotional experiences and not something that prompts a strong reaction. An example might be, you are driving and you almost hit something in front of you. *Barely missing the parked car left me feeling anxious.*

Go to the list of painful feelings and read the words out loud. Identify words that associate with the way you are feeling. If you find this to be difficult, just use a word that describes something you have observed before or how you think someone you know might feel in that same situation. You may even ask them if you would like. It doesn't have to be perfect; the point is to practice until naming the emotions you feel is comfortable for you.

Painful Feelings

Abandoned	Angry	Anxious
Ashamed	Bad	Betrayed
Broken	Bullied	Cheated
Confused	Controlled	Criticized
Depressed	Desperate	Discouraged
Disposable	Embarrassed	Excluded
Exhausted	Exposed	Forgotten
Frightened	Frustrated	Furious
Grief stricken	Guilty	Heartbroken
Helpless	Hurt	Ignored
In the way	Insecure	Jealous
Judged	Left out	Lied to
Lonely	Lost	Manipulated
Misplaced	Mistreated	Misunderstood
Nagged	Nervous	Numb
Overwhelmed	Offended	Pathetic
Picked on	Pissed off	Powerless
Rejected	Resented	Resentful
Ridiculed	Sad	Scared

Self-conscious
Skeptical
Threatened
Tired
Traumatized
Troubled
Undervalued
Unwanted
Unworthy
Useless
Victimized
Vindictive
Violated
Vulnerable
Worthless

There is no right or wrong way to feel, so stay out of any judgment and give yourself permission to acknowledge and accept that having and expressing emotions is a normal part of life.

Based on the information I have gained, I will take these three actions to understand my emotions, strengthen my relationships, and make my life more meaningful.

1. ____________________

2. ____________________

3.

Self-Discovery Notes

Day Nineteen

Getting Offended and Taking Things Personally

Taking Things Personally

The purpose of this process is to help you acknowledge and accept the negative impact that getting offended or taking things personally has had on your life.

- What types of comments do I take personally?
- When I am offended, or take something personally, I usually (*Blame others; Enroll others in my drama to justify my actions; Lash out; Lie to avoid any consequences; Transfer my irritation to someone else not involved in the situation like a spouse, child, or neighbor's dog; Withdraw, sulk, or act out to avoid dealing with what is really going on.)*
- What and/or Who offends me?
- What is my typical behavior when I am offended or take something personally?
- How does blaming others affect my ability to feel loved in relationships?
- When something or someone offends me, what is a typical story I make up to justify my reaction?

Based on the information I have gained, I will take these three actions to get beyond "taking things personally", strengthen my relationships, and make my life more meaningful.

1. ____

   ____

2. ______________________________

3. ______________________________

Self-Discovery Notes ______________________________

Day Twenty

Beauty from Pain

Stepping Out of Pain into a Beautiful Life

The purpose of this process is to identify the beauty lost through painful memories.

- What _________ *(memory, loss, relationship)* have I had a hard time getting over?
- With that loss, what do I regret? What do I miss?
- What do I wish I would have said?
- What has this loss taught me?
- What pleasant memories would I like to retain from this experience?
- How has this loss been beneficial to my learning and growth?

Based on the information I have gained, I will take these three actions to eliminate my pain, create more beauty in my relationships, and make my life more meaningful.

1. ____

2.

3.

Self-Discovery Notes

Day Twenty-One

From Self-Doubt to Self-Discovery

From Self-Doubt to Self-Discovery

The purpose of this process is to let go of doubt and discover the power within to manage, control, and change your life.

- What painful memory have I had a hard time getting over?
- How can I reframe that memory to remember what I enjoyed, rather than what I lost? *(I remind myself how he loved me, not how he left me.)*
- Where do I feel I never quite "measure up"? (*with my boss, raising children, with my significant other's co-workers.*)
- Where are the areas in my life I have a hard time coping, but tell others I'm doing just fine?
- With what detrimental feelings do I struggle most?
- What have these detrimental feelings taught me about myself? *(You are braver than you believe, stronger than you seem, and smarter than you think. ~ "Winnie the Pooh")*
- What are my secret insecurities?
- What are my greatest strengths?

You have all the power you need to change the feelings that you have about yourself. A good way to attach your strengths with empowering feelings is to take what you have just written and, at least ten times a day, repeat to yourself "I am _________ (*deserving*)." You will quickly notice changes in the way you feel. This will give you more freedom to feel _________ (*deserving*) in every area of your life. Reinforce your feelings by thinking of ways in your life where you are _________ *(deserving)*. You can use this process any time you want to boost your confidence or success. Try it now, look up, smile, take a deep breath, and say in a loud voice "I feel deserving and appreciated!" Feels great, doesn't it!

Another tool you can use to go from self-doubt to self-discovery is to appreciate the things you have learned about yourself, by writing yourself a personal letter. Acknowledge the accomplishments you have achieved such as; obstacles you have overcome, ways you have enhanced the lives of others, talents you have developed and things of which you are proud.

A letter to my amazing self, ______________________________

____

____

____

____

____

____

____

____

____

Get note cards and ask people you know to write attributes, experiences, or actions that they appreciate about you. Keep the cards with your letter.

When doubt starts to creep in, having evidence that refutes detrimental self-talk and disparaging feelings and beliefs will make a difference.

Based on the information I have gained, I will take these three actions to stop my doubt, discover my strengths, enhance my relationships, and create more meaning in my life.

1. ______________________________

2. ______________________________

3. ______________________________

Self-Discovery Notes

Day Twenty-Two

The Power of Forgiveness

The Power of Forgiveness

The purpose of this process is to gain a deeper understanding of why you protect yourself by holding on to pain, sorrow, or resentment. This awareness will increase your ability to let go of the past and introduce a happier future.

When we choose to forgive, we release the emotional connection others hold over our lives.

Recall thoughts, feelings, attitudes, and beliefs that prevent you from forgiving yourself or others. Then ask,

- Specifically, what am I hanging on to?
- What pain in my life requires forgiveness?
- For what do I need to forgive myself?
- Why is this hard to me?
- What price have I paid for hanging on to this pain, sorrow, hate, or resentment?
- How will letting go of burdens I carry towards ________ benefit my life?

Based on the information I have gained, I will take these three actions to forgive myself and others, strengthen my relationships, and make my life more meaningful.

1. ____

   ____

   ____

2.

3.

Self-Discovery Notes

Day Twenty-Three

The Road to Self-Acceptance

Love and Acceptance

The purpose of this process is to move from being critical with ourselves to creating practices that will support feelings of self-love and acceptance.

- What is the biggest barrier that holds me back from accepting myself?
- From where do I believe this challenge comes? *(Something I have heard over and over again. Something that I say to myself over and over again?)*
- In what areas of my life do I need to acknowledge and forgive myself?
- What attitudes make it hard to love and accept myself?
- In what areas of life do I want to feel at peace with myself?
- What do I value about myself?
- In what ways am I entirely unique?
- How would I describe the person people don't see?
- In what ways do I take care of myself? *(Emotionally, physically, socially, financially, intellectually, etc…)*

Keep an "I Am totally Awesome" journal to acknowledge great things about yourself and your life on a daily basis.

I Am
totally
Awesome

Based on the information I have gained, I will take these three actions to increase feelings of self-love, strengthen my relationships, and make my life more meaningful?

1. ____

2. ____

3. ____

Self-Discovery Notes

Day Twenty-Four

Trusting Yourself

Trusting your Inner Judgment

The purpose of this process is to recognize areas in your life where you trust yourself, and areas where you would like to improve your trust, thoughts, or actions.

Trusting yourself begins with little steps. Making commitments and keeping them, whether with yourself or others, is an essential process in developing trusting relationships.

How well do I keep the commitments I make to myself? *(I'm going to lose 30 pounds, I'm going to work out 3 times a week, I'm going to take a vacation.)*

- In what areas of my life do I trust my decisions?
- What experiences have caused me to doubt myself?
- How has a lack of trust in myself impacted my life?
- How has a lack of trust impacted the way I feel about myself?
- How has a lack of trust in myself impacted my relationships?
- How has a lack of trust in myself impacted my education?
- How has a lack of trust impacted my employment?

When you trust yourself, you gain the self-assurance to take risks, confidence to create successful relationships and the passion needed to attain success.

Self-trust allows you to feel and follow the inner strength that guides your path.

Here is a technique that will help you clarify your internal instincts:

> Close your eyes and relax. Think of something you really enjoy. Stay relaxed until you are aware of how wonderful it feels to sit and enjoy _________ *(What you really enjoy)* in your life.
>
> Open your eyes and process what you felt and where you felt it.
>
> For example, "I thought of a memory with someone I love and…
>
> "I had a warm feeling in my heart." "There was a rush of joy that filled my chest." "I had butterflies in my stomach."
>
> Write what you felt and where you felt it. *(Mind, stomach, heart.)*
>
> Recognizing these feelings and where you hold them will help you decipher when you know something is right.
>
> Now let's look at fear. Think of an event where you felt fear. Stay focused until you are aware of how it felt when you were thrown into a state of fear. Process what you felt and where you felt it. For example, I saw a snake on the trail and…
>
> "I felt sick to my stomach." "I felt anxiety in my chest, upper arms, or the back of my neck." "I felt panic." "My breathing increased, my chest became tight, and my heart began to race." "I was afraid, the hair on my arms stood up, and I felt 'the chills.'"
>
> Write what you feel and where you feel it:

The place in the mind that processes emotion is unaware of what we see and what we remember. As a result, it can easily produce an emotion based on our thoughts. As such, you can use this same process to identify happiness, sadness, or other types of emotions.

Continue the process by finishing the following sentences:

- Whom do I trust?
- Who in my life trusts me?
- How will honest communication improve my level of trust?
- How will I know when I trust myself?
- How will the relationships in my life get better when I can trust myself?
- What other things in my life will improve when I know I can trust myself?

Based on the information I have gained, I will take these three actions to increase self-trust, strengthen my relationships and, make my life more meaningful?

1. ______________________________

2. ______________________________

3.

Self-Discovery Notes

Day Twenty-Five

Clarifying Values

Clarifying Values

The purpose of this process is to assist you in identifying and understanding the things in your life that are the foundation of your values.

To start the process, use the chart to determine where you spend the majority of your time.

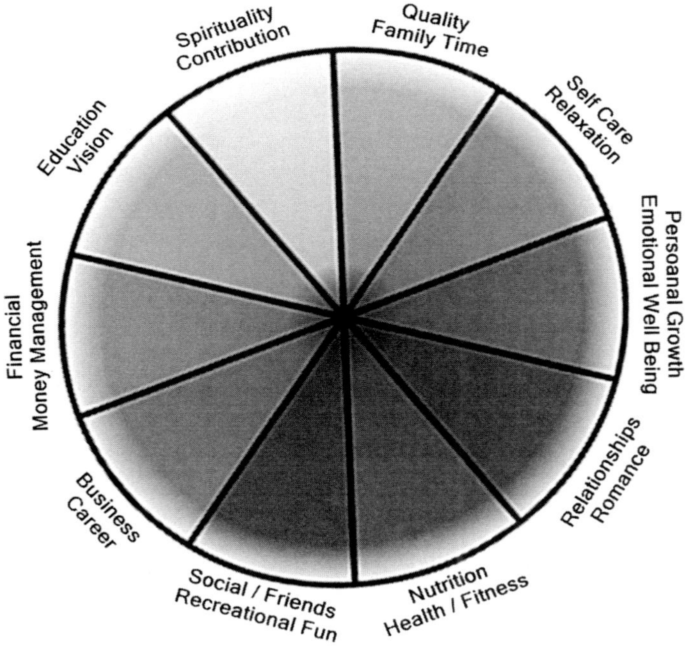

Category	Time Spent
Quality Family Time	
Spirituality / Contribution	
Self Care / Relaxation	
Personal Growth / Emotional Well Being	
Relationships / Romance	
Nutrition Health / Fitness	
Social / Friends Recreation / Fun	
Business / Career	
Financial / Money Management	
Education / Vision	

Now take some time to define the value you place in different aspects of your life.

- What does my optimal mental/emotional well-being include?
- What does my optimal physical well-being include?
- What does my optimal spiritual well-being include?
- What does my optimal social well-being include?
- What does my ideal relationship/romantic life include?
- What does my personal growth include?
- What does my ideal education include?
- What does my ideal living environment include?
- What does my ideal financial condition include?
- What does my ideal profession include?
- What does my ideal fun and recreational life include?
- What five things do I value most?
- What do I value about these five things?

(For example; Value 1: I value self-sufficiency.)

How do I define these values?

The definition of _________ *(self-sufficiency)* is _________ *(having the confidence to trust my own ability to care for my needs and the needs of my family).*

- How will I incorporate these values into my life?
- What agreements will I make to integrate common values into my close relationships?
- What personal strengths do I value in myself?
- What personal character traits do I value? *(Don't forget the qualities you defined in day thirteen.)*

Based on the information I have gained, I will take these three actions to establish my values, strengthen relationships, and make my life more meaningful.

1. ____________________

2. ____________________

3. ____________________

Self-Discovery Notes

Day Twenty-Six

Overcoming Obstacles

Overcome Obstacles

The purpose of this process is to help you clarify, detail, and overcome the obstacles that get in the way of your happiness and growth.

- Begin by clarifying an obstacle.
- What specific obstacles am I facing?
- What am I trying to control?
- What is outside of my ability to control?
- What must I surrender? (*Being right; Controlling others; I can't change the past.*)
- What fears influence my ability to surrender?
- What self-talk do I use against myself or the situation that prevents me from moving forward?
- What part of this obstacle do I believe I cannot handle?
- What lessons can I learn from the obstacles I am facing? *(Having extra weight helps me focus on a healthy living style.)*
- What is the greatest obstacle I have faced and overcome?
- What has overcoming my obstacles given me the ability to create?

Based on the information I have gained, I will take these three actions to overcome obstacles, strengthen my relationships, and create a more meaningful life.

1.

2.

3.

Self-Discovery Notes

Day Twenty-Seven

The Master of Emotions

Mastering Emotions

The purpose of this process is to look at the journey of self-discovery and understand what it will take for you to become the master of your emotions.

Mastering our emotions includes the ability to logically process emotional events.

As you ponder an emotionally-charged event contemplate your thoughts, feelings, behaviors, and your reaction.

- Describe the event.
- What were my prominent feelings?
- When I was in an emotional state, what was my logic?
- How did my logic affect my action or inaction?
- How much of my logic was influenced by an underlying belief? Name the belief.
- What did I notice about my behavior? *(Anytime I am around someone who is angry I get nervous; I fight; I freeze; I withdraw; I walk away.)*
- How are the emotional events in my past affecting my perception?
- How have I blamed others for my circumstances or behaviors?
- From where is the intensity of my feelings coming?
- In what ways do I avoid looking at my emotional and behavioral patterns?
- How do my emotions affect my physical body?

When you notice a fear, question the logic of that fear.

- What do I fear?
- From where do I believe my fears are coming?
- How long have I held these fears?
- How do my fears limit me?
- How relevant are these fears to my current situation or life?

Ponder your reaction and notice the emotional patterns; In other words, consciously link your feelings in this situation with other times you have felt this way.

- What common factors trigger me?
- What underlying beliefs control my doubts?
- What is the biggest discovery I have made about my emotional perceptions?
- How will this discovery improve my life?

Based on the information I have gained, I will take these three actions to master my emotions, strengthen my relationships, and make my life more meaningful.

1. ______________________________

2. ________________

3. ________________

Self-Discovery Notes ________________

Day Twenty-Eight

The Force Within

Acknowledge the Journey

The purpose of this process is to acknowledge the self-discovery tools you have gained to overcome the emotional barriers that keep you in a victim mentality.

- Over the past several weeks what has been my greatest discovery?
- What is the most insightful thing that I have learned about myself?
- What have I noticed about myself when I feel hurt, offended, or have taken something personally?
- When I am offended how do I typically justify my actions?
- When I am struggling, what underlying beliefs have the most power over me?
- What defense mechanisms do I most often use to protect myself?
- What have I discovered about my coping mechanisms?
- Where am I most likely to get offended or take something personally?
- In what circumstances/experiences do I tolerate being mistreated?
- Who is the person I react to the most?
- What has been my experience with this person?
- How is this person tied to my history? *(They remind me of how I was treated as a child; Times when I felt inadequate; A painful relationship)*

- What fears have the most control over me?
- What have I changed to get out of my comfort zone?

Based on the information I have gained, I will take these three actions to understand my victim mentality, strengthen my relationships, and make my life more meaningful.

1. ______________________________

2. ______________________________

3. ______________________________

Self-Discovery Notes

Day Twenty-Nine

Living an Accountable Life

Living an Accountable Life

The purpose of this process is to increase your understanding of how to take personal ownership of the choices you make and to live an accountable life.

- In what ways has taking ownership for the choices that I make changed my perspective?
- In what ways do I value myself?
- In what ways do I ask for what I want?
- When I feel emotion, what thoughts help me progress from feeling powerless to powerful?
- How well do I honestly and effectively express myself?
- When I make a mistake that hurts another, how do I rectify the problem?
- How can I be a better listener?
- In what areas of my life am I open to the perspectives and ideas of others?
- When I experience a conflict, how do I typically handle it?
- What do I appreciate about challenging situations in my life?
- How do I know that the way I am approaching a conflict is working?
- In what areas in life am I generating the result that I want?
- How am I contributing to the lives of others?
- How will the discoveries I have made give me the power to manage, control, and change my emotions and my life?

Based on the information I have gained, I will take these three actions to increase accountability, strengthen relationships, and make my life more meaningful.

1. ____

2. ____

3. ____

Self-Discovery Notes

Day Thirty

Accessing Your Inner Motivation to Succeed

The next subject that we are going to address is how to activate all that you have learned by consciously connecting what you see and how you feel to what you want to create through positive affirmations, mind maps, and vision boards.

Before we begin, I would like to give you a brief explanation of why motivational speakers feel that positive affirmations, mind maps, and vision boards are so effective. Many motivational speakers use the models and techniques of NLP or *Neuro-Linguistic Programming. Neuro-Linguistic Programming describes the fundamental dynamics between mind *(neuro)* and language *(linguistic)*, and how their interplay affects our body and behavior *(programming)**.

(*NLP definition given by Robert Dilts http://www.nlpu.com/NewDesign/NLPU_WhatIsNLP.html)

The questions and processes throughout this book have been designed to help you redirect the neurological configurations and linguistic structures that form the emotional habits of your mind so you can create profound changes easily and quickly. Positive affirmations, mind maps, and vision boards are a fun way to motivate action and implement the changes you seek to make.

Engaging your Inner Motivation to Succeed

On his website at http://jackcanfield.com/affirmations/ Jack Canfield gives five guidelines to follow when creating powerful affirmations.

1. Start by entering the present tense. In other words, take the condition you desire and declare it as if it were already true.
2. Be positive. Place emphasis on what you want. For example: saying, "I want to quit smoking," would keep the focus on smoking, versus, "I want to live a life that is smoke-free," which changes the focus from what is not wanted (smoking) to what is wanted (living a smoke-free life).
3. Be concise. The shorter the better. Affirmations with fewer words are often easier to recall. Rhyming makes your affirmations even more memorable. For example, "I am feeling alive at 185."
4. Include action. Whenever possible, affirm yourself as a person who takes action. For example: "I am gratefully driving my new Porsche along an open highway." Action engages the Law of Attraction, creating new results in our lives and opening us to further inspiration.
5. Include a feeling word. Powerful affirmations include content and emotion. Content describes the specific outcome that you desire. Emotion gets to the heart of how you feel about that outcome.
6. Create "I am" statements. I once heard Canfield say that creating "I am" statements that take charge of your results is a very effective way to create powerful affirmations. Here is one of my favorites. "I am Creating Balance and Feeling Peaceful in all areas of My Life!"

Mind mapping is another way you can connect what you want with what you see and the action that you take. Here is a fun idea for mind mapping that ties positive affirmations and mind mapping together.

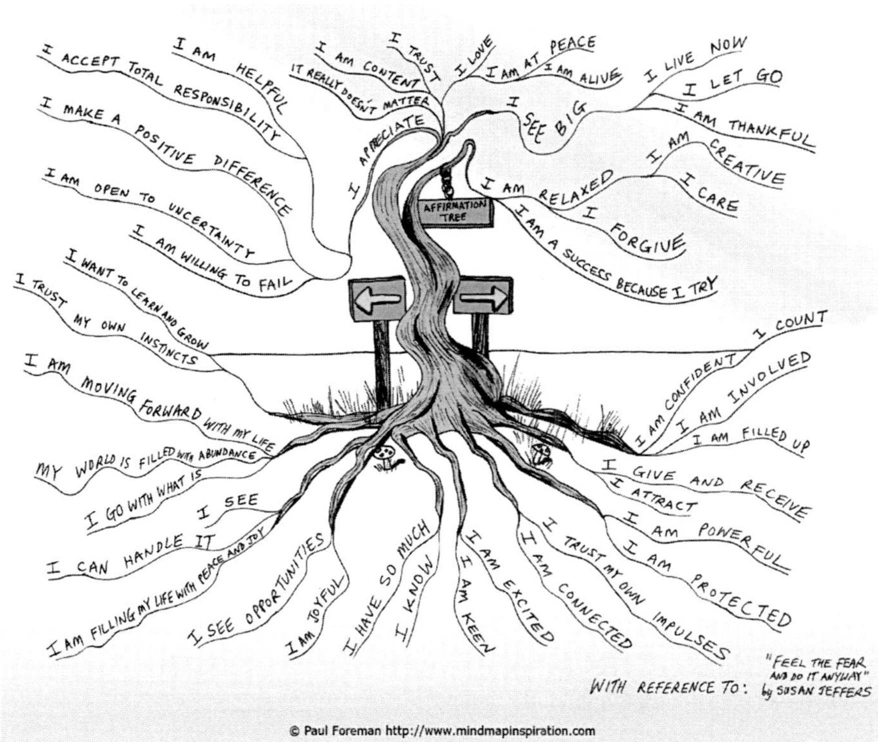

Here is a basic overview to guide you through mind mapping.

Five Stages of Mind Mapping

1. Determine your goal: Here are some suggestions of areas you might consider and questions you could ask to help you clarify your direction.

   Areas to consider:

   - Health: Physical / Mental / Emotional
   - Relationships: Family / Friendships / Romantic / Others
   - Communication: Where I feel understood / Areas I would like to improve
   - Growth: Personal / Spiritual / Educational

- Social: Personal interaction / Social media interaction
- Happiness: Recreation / Relaxation / Hobbies / Fun
- Career: Business / Advances / Change
- Finances: Money / Earning / Spending / Saving
- Contribution: Areas I contribute / Areas I would like to expand

Questions you could ask:

- What I enjoy about my _________ is *(Example: What I enjoy about my physical health is (_________)* ____________________

  ____

  ____

  ____

  ____

  ____

- What I would like to improve in my life is ______________

  ____

  ____

  ____

  ____

  ____

- How I would like my outcome to be is (*How it will look when you have accomplished your goal.)* ______________________

  ____

  ____

  ____

  ____

2. Analyze where you are and what you are trying to achieve

   In my training *The Power to Change* I use a version of the SMART Goal formula to identify goals.

   - **S**pecific: Detail what you are trying to achieve.
   - **M**easurable: What benchmarks will you use to measure your progress?
   - **A**ction: What daily action can you take to accomplish your goal?
   - **R**ealistic: Is your goal realistic for your current life?
   - **T**imely: When is the deadline to achieve this goal? It is also helpful to set timelines for little accomplishments you want to experience along the way.

   Take time to reward yourself when little goals have been accomplished and celebrate when you have achieved your desired result. When you celebrate your successes, it connects your accomplishments to the reward center of the mind, which will increase your energy and excitement for new endeavors.

3. Chunk it Down Through Mapping

   Now that you have specific goals, you can map what needs to be done. This is also the stage where you will

   - Prioritize the resources you will use,
   - Clarify the people you will contact,
   - Identify the action steps you will take, and
   - Determine the timeline you will follow to accomplish your final objective.

4. Take Action

   Mapping should be done in a way that piques your enthusiasm every time you visualize your objectives. Don't be afraid to expand or update new ideas. Just be careful that you don't over complicate the process. Stay focused on step-by-step action items that will create excitement as you move closer to your goal.

5. Celebrate

   The ultimate goal is to create the life you want. It will be much easier to do if you connect your small accomplishments with the reward center of your brain by experiencing pleasure along the way. So, take the limits off! Get out of any logical boundaries you have placed upon yourself and create goals that are outrageous and fun! If you can conceive it and you are willing to take daily steps towards it, you will achieve it! Remember, when you engage the passion of your heart and the power of your mind together, your potential becomes limitless!

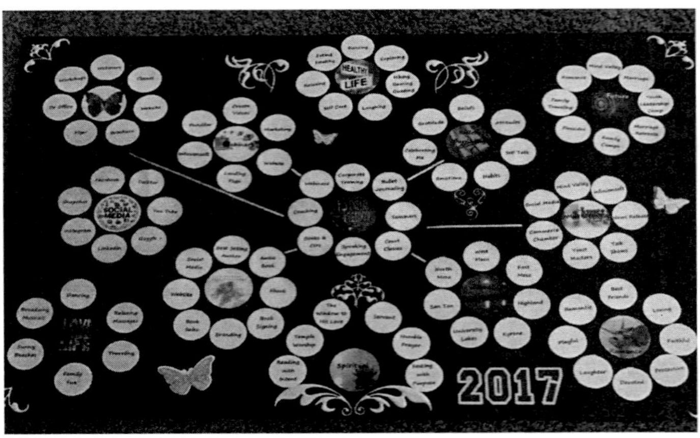

This is a picture of my motivational mind map for 2017

Vision Board

The third tool will be to create a vision board. A vision board is where you visually connect to the outcomes you desire. The fun thing about creating a vision board is that you put it together as if you were living your dream now. One of the dreams I have is creating a leadership camp for impoverished youth called *The Power Within.* I know exactly what I want it to include. So, when I was creating my vision board, I found a lot of images of youth getting beyond the limits of their fears as they participate in a high-energy ropes course. I also have pictures of youth working together to overcome obstacles in outdoor team-building activities. My dream is to include multiple motivational trainers, including myself, to give these young people powerful tools and confidence to create a happy and successful life. I would like image consultants, educational scholarship specialists, and business mentors to donate their time and talents to help these young people take their lives on in a whole new way. Other things on my vision board include family fun, hot tubbing in the snow, lying on the beach, horseback riding, relaxing massages, and fun with family and friends. There are also pictures of the vision I have for my business and me standing in front of a TED audience sharing my passion of emotional perceptions.

As you can see, my vision board is a constant reminder that connects my vision with the excitement and inner motivation I need to succeed. It's exciting to realize the daily progress of making my dreams come true.

This has been such a wonderful journey! Thank you for the opportunity to share what I have learned throughout my life with you. You have all the power you need to live a rich and fulfilling life. It is my hope that you don't just hope that your life will change, but that you will take the necessary actions, get curious about your emotional reactions and decide to make the changes necessary to create a life full of happiness and peace. If I can do it, so can you!

If you read the book 30 Days Through Self Discovery you have already read this, but for those who have not purchased the book I would like to share a delightful story I was given permission to use, by author Michael D. Hargrove and Bottom Line Underwriters, Inc.

Don't Hope ... Decide

While waiting to pick up a friend at the airport in Portland, Oregon, I had one of those life-changing experiences that you hear other people talk about, the kind that sneaks up on you unexpectedly. This one occurred a mere two feet away from me. Straining to locate my friend among the passengers deplaning through the jet way, I noticed a man coming toward me carrying small bags.

He stopped right next to me to greet his family. First, he motioned to his youngest son (who looked to be about six years old) as he put down his bags. They gave each other a long, loving hug. As they separated enough to look into each other's faces, I heard the father say, "It's so good to see you, son. I missed you so much!" His son smiled somewhat shyly, averted his eyes and replied softly, "Me, too, Dad!"

Then the man stood up, gazed in the eyes of his oldest son (who was probably nine or ten) and, while cupping his son's face in his hands, said, "You're already quite the young man. I love you very much, Zach!" They too exchanged a most loving, tender hug.

While this was happening, a baby girl (perhaps one or one-and-a-half) was squirming excitedly in her mother's arms, never once taking her little eyes off the wonderful sight of her returning father.

The man said, "Hi, baby girl!" as he gently took the child from her mother. He quickly kissed her face all over and then held her close to his chest while rocking her from side to side. The little girl instantly relaxed and simply laid her head on his shoulder, motionless, in pure contentment.

After several moments, he handed his daughter to his oldest son and declared, "I've saved the best for last!" and proceeded to give his wife the longest, most passionate kiss I ever remember seeing.

He gazed into her eyes for several seconds and then silently mouthed. "I love you so much!" They stared at each other's eyes, beaming big smiles at one another while holding both hands. For an instant, they reminded me of newlyweds, but I knew by the age of their children that they couldn't possibly be.

I puzzled about it for a moment, then realized how totally engrossed I was in the wonderful display of unconditional love not more than an arm's length away from me.

I suddenly felt uncomfortable, as if I was invading something sacred, so I was amazed to hear my own voice nervously ask, "Wow! How long have you two been married?"

"Been together fourteen years' total, married twelve of those," the man replied, without breaking his gaze from his lovely wife's face.

"Well then, how long have you been away?" I asked the man.

He finally turned and looked at me, still beaming his joyous smile. "Two whole days!" he said.

Two days? I was stunned. By the intensity of the greeting, I had assumed he'd been gone for at least several weeks, if not months. I know my expression betrayed me; I said, almost off- handedly, hoping to end my intrusion with some semblance of grace (and to get back to searching for my friend), "I hope my marriage is still that passionate after twelve years!"

The man suddenly stopped smiling. He looked me straight in the eye, and with a forcefulness that burned right into my soul, he told me something that left me a different person. He told me, "Don't hope, friend … decide!" Then he flashed me his wonderful smile again, shook my hand and said, "God bless!" With that, he and his family turned and strode away together. I was still watching that exceptional man and his special family walk just out of sight when my friend came up to me and asked, "What'cha looking at?" Without hesitating, and with a curious sense of certainty, I replied, "My future!"

As you design your future, don't just hope for the changes you seek decide to make a conscious effort to change the unconscious ways you have been giving your power away. Get beyond unconscious emotional patterns and instead, live the life that you have always dreamed!

Remember, "DON'T HOPE, FRIEND, DECIDE!"